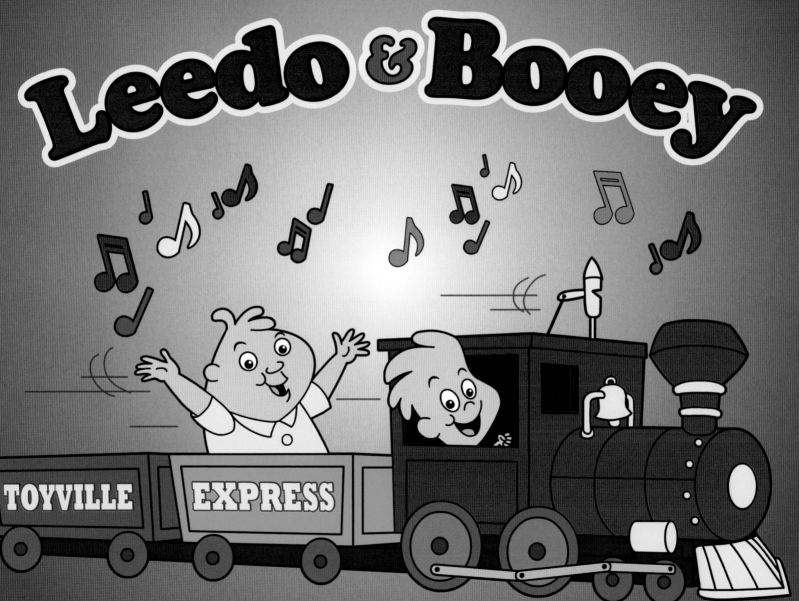

ISBN 978-1-937359-45-4
Library of Congress Control Number: 2013932997
The Library of Congress has catalogued the hardcover edition as follows: Leedo & Booey / Dr. Gart

Published by

www.gartunes.com

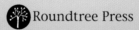 Roundtree Press

6 Petaluma Blvd. North, Suite B-6 Petaluma, CA 94952

Distributed by Publishers Group West, 1700 Fourth Street, Berkeley CA 94710   Printed in China

Join LEEDO & BOOEY's Fan Club for more surprises at:
www.leedoandbooey.com

SING ALONG WITH
Leedo & Booey

Words and Music by
Dr. Gart

Illustrated by
Layron DeJarnette

PART ONE
Words & Pictures
Read & Sing Along with your CD

PART TWO
Music & Lyrics
Bonus Sheet Music to Sing & Play Along

PART ONE
Words & Pictures

Introducing...

Leedo Booey

Hey Kids!

Join the adventures of Leedo and Booey,
come meet their funny Papa named Looey.
Look in and listen to all that they do,
they'll bring lots of fun and laughter to you.

When the sun comes up to start their day,
they wash and dress, and then they play.
They walk their dog, they ride their bike,
they help Mom shop for things they like.

Then quick as a flash, they're off for a ride,
on a bus or a train, then down the slide.
They go to school and make up rhymes,
so sing along and share good times.

Fifteen songs, they're easy to learn,
with teachers and friends, you can all take a turn.
You'll smile at each picture, right from the start,
with words and music by Dr. Gart.

Doggy

There are no words to sing along,
just funny sounds make up this song.

Barump

Barump

Peem Pom Bom Boom Bom Bay

Rump

Peem Pom Bom Boom Bom Bay

Rump

Peem Pom Bom Boom Bom Boom Bom Bay

Oh Oh Oh Oh

Boopetty Poopy Doopy Day

Bahdum Bahdum Bahdoom Bom Bay

SONG
1

The sun comes up to start the day,
now don't waste time, so we can play.

Brand New Day

I wake up in the morning and I brush my teeth,
the front and back, top and underneath.
I wash my hands and face and everything's okay,
getting ready for a brand new day.

I put away my toys and help to make my bed,
then clean my room like my mommy said.
I have some toast and jelly, then it's time to play,
getting ready for a brand new day.

'Cause, everyday is a new day.
A fun day. Sky is blue day.
Yes, everyday's a me and you day.
Getting ready for a brand new day.

I pick a pair of pants and then a shirt to match,
my favorite socks mommy needs to patch.
I tie up both my shoes and then I'm on my way,
getting ready for a brand new day.

'Cause, everyday is a new day.
A fun day. Sky is blue day.
Yes, everyday's a me and you day.
Getting ready for a brand new day.

GETTING READY FOR
A BRAND NEW DAY!

SONG
2

Hold that smile, count to three,
our picture-perfect family.

Family

Mommy, Daddy, Grampa, Grammy,
all a part of family.
Fathers, mothers, sisters, brothers,
aunts and uncles, then there's me.

A family gets bigger when babies join the world.
It's fun to try and figure, if it's a boy or girl.

Mommy, Daddy, Grampa, Grammy,
all a part of family.
Fathers, mothers, sisters, brothers,
aunts and uncles, then there's me.

A family gets bigger when babies join the world.
It's fun to try and figure if it's a boy or girl.

Mommy, Daddy, Grampa, Grammy,
all a part of family.
Fathers, mothers, sisters, brothers,
aunts and uncles, then there's me!

SONG
3

We teach our doggy lots of tricks,
to jump and catch, and pick up sticks.

That's My Doggy

My doggy always protects me,
from anyone who comes my way.

She sits at home
with her ball and bone,
waiting till I'm back to play.

That's my doggy,
she's my buddy, she's my friend.
That's my doggy,
and she'll be here till the end.
That's my doggy,
I'm so proud to call her mine.
That's my doggy,
so fine!

We go for walks in the afternoon,
soon as I get home from school.

She wags her tail
as we pick a trail,
back for dinner is the rule.

That's my doggy,
she's my buddy, she's my friend.
That's my doggy,
and she'll be here till the end.
That's my doggy,
I'm so proud to call her mine.
That's my doggy,
so fine!

SONG
4

Lots of rhythm, fingers snapping,
music playing, hands are clapping.

Finger Song

Fee, Fi, Fo, Fum,
Little, Ring, Middle, Pointer, Thumb.
Counting fingers one by one.
Clap your hands and have some fun.

The Pinky is the little.
The Ring is next in line.
The long one's in the middle.
The Pointer then you'll find.

Fee, Fi, Fo, Fum,
Last but not least Mister Thumb.
Counting fingers one by one.
Clap your hands and have some fun.

Fee, Fi, Fo, Fum,
Little, Ring, Middle, Pointer, Thumb.
Counting fingers one by one.
Clap your hands and have some fun!

SONG
5

If you love Leedo and you love Booey,
then sing along with Papa Looey.

Daddy's Song

Listen everybody to my
Daddy's favorite song.
Yidel deedle dydel dum,
he sings the whole day long.

Yidel deedle dydel dum,
the words don't mean a thing.
Yidel deedle dydel dum,
but happiness they bring.

Listen everybody to my
Daddy's favorite song.
Yidel deedle dydel dum,
it's not so very long.

Yidel deedle dydel dum,
will chase away the rain.
Yidel deedle dydel dum,
on Cherry Blossom Lane.

Yidel deedle dydel dum,
a happy melody.
Yidel deedle dydel dum,
in three part harmony.

Listen everybody to my
Daddy's favorite song.
Yidel deedle dydel dum,
it's fun to sing along.

Yidel deedle dydel dum,
they're magic words to say.
Yidel deedle dydel dum,
will brighten up your day!

SONG
6

Wave good-bye, then off to school,
learning stuff is pretty cool.

Schooltime

School Time, School Time.
Grab your books and take the bus.
School Time, School Time.
What a time for all of us.

If you have a thought that's on your mind,
put it in a question then you'll find.
Raise your hand in class,
then wait until your turn.
If you never ask you'll never learn.

School Time, School Time.
Grab your books and take the bus.
School Time, School Time.
What a time for all of us.

If you find your homework's hard for you,
tell ya what I think you ought to do.
See if you can get help from your family.
You can solve the problem easily.

If you have to do a show and tell,
share a story that you know so well.
Bring along a picture, or a special toy.
Make it fun for every girl and boy.

School Time, School Time.
Grab your books and take the bus.
School Time, School Time.
What a time for all of us.

What a time for all of us!

SONG
7

Push the wagon, fill the cart,
let's buy some food for Dr. Gart.

Shopping Cart

I like sitting in the shopping cart,
picking food up at the supermart.
Mommy pushes me around the store,
I find everything we're looking for.

Up and down the aisles we go,
back and forth and to and fro.
Crossing off the list we bring,
checking we don't miss a thing.

First stop's one to get some gum to chew,
juice and milk we get on aisle two.
Fruits and vegetables on three and four,
aisle five's behind a freezer door.

Up and down the aisles we go,
back and forth and to and fro.
Crossing off the list we bring,
checking we don't miss a thing.

Next my favorite aisle, number six,
lots of cookies and some pretzel sticks.
Seven, eight, spaghetti sauce on nine,
down aisle ten into the checkout line.

Up and down the aisles we go,
back and forth and to and fro.
Crossing off the list we bring,
checking we don't miss a thing.

Oh how fun to go shopping!

Shopping List
Cereal
Soup
Bread
Milk
Lunch Meat
Crackers

SONG
8

Climb the bars, then swing so high,
just point your toes up to the sky.

The Playground

The playground is a place for kids,
to run and jump and swing.
The playground is a place for kids,
to do most anything.

Climb way up top the sliding pond,
then tumble to the ground.
If anybody wants to know,
it's here I can be found.

The playground is a place for kids,
to come and meet new friends.
The playground is a place for kids,
the fun just never ends.

Swing clear across the monkey bars,
away up in the sky.
The see-saw is a game for two,
so why not give a try?

Climb way up top the sliding pond,
then tumble to the ground.
If anybody wants to know,
it's here I can be found.

The playground is a place for kids,
it's open every day.
The playground is a place for kids,
so come with me and play!

SONG
9

The weatherman said, "There'll be no rain."
Let's climb aboard the choo-choo train.

Train Song

Yee Hee Hee
Yee Haw Ha

Yee Hee Hee
Ooh Ah Ha

Yoo Hoo Hoo
Ah Ha Ha

Yee Hee Hee
Ooh Ah Ha

SONG
10

Pedal, pedal little feet.
Stay on the path, not in the street!

My Bicycle

You may like to skip-to-my-loo,
or run and jump in playschool.
But there is one thing I like to do,
all the live-long day through.

I like to ride my bicycle.
I like to ride my bike.

I remember learning to ride,
back when I was seven.
My seat was fat, my tires were wide.
Did I forget to mention?

I like to ride my bicycle.
I like to ride my bike.
I like to ride my bicycle.
I like to ride my bike.

Bicycle Rider.
I like to ride my bicycle.
I like to ride my bike.

SONG
11

Caught my finger in the door,
now my thumb is really sore.

Owwee

Owwee, owwee, oh meowee,
what else can I say?
Owwee, owwee, oh meowee,
make it go away.

Sometimes you're outside playing, and dirt gets in your eye.
A sting and burn and then you learn, you try hard not to cry.

Owwee, owwee, oh meowee,
what else can I say?
Owwee, owwee, oh meowee,
make it go away.

So if you get a boo-boo, and scrape your hands and knees,
A sting and burn, and then you learn, be careful climbing trees.

Owwee, owwee, oh meowee,
what else can I say?
Owwee, owwee, oh meowee,
make it go away.

SONG
12

Bubbles, bubbles, so much fun.
Poke and pop them, one by one.

Bubbles

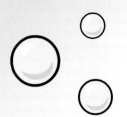

Bubbles, bubbles in my tub,
they're floating everywhere.

Poke and pop 'em if you can,
before they disappear.

I like to splish and splash
in a bubbly world of snow.

I like to laugh and play
with my ducky and my boat.

Scrub-a-dub it's fun to wash
with all my friends around.
Here's a small one,
there's a tall one,
shiny and so round.

I like to splish and splash
in a bubbly world of snow.

I like to laugh and play
with my ducky and my boat.

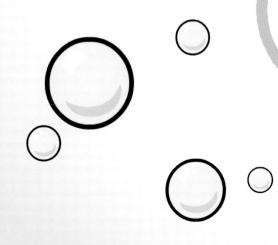

SONG
13

SPECIAL
2 SCOOPS
FOR 1

CHOCOLATE

VANILLA

The chocolate's all gone, now don't be sad.
Try the vanilla, it's not so bad.

What Goes Up

What goes up, must come down.
It's when a smile becomes a frown.

Look at things from upside down,
and they will turn around.

My friend Matt had a cat,
but then one day she ran away.
Matt got sad, was feeling bad,
then his kitty came back to play.

What goes up must come down.
It's when a smile becomes a frown.

Look at things from upside down,
and they will turn around.

Cousin Mike broke his bike,
it wouldn't ride, and so he cried.
After school Dad found a tool,
and fixed its broken side.

What goes up must come down.
It's when a smile becomes a frown.

Look at things from upside down,
and they will turn around.

Peggy Sue caught the flu,
stayed at home and felt alone.
Her best friend helped her mend,
and cheered her on the phone.

What goes up must come down.
It's when a smile becomes a frown.

Look at things from upside down,
and they will turn,
oh yes they'll turn,
and they will turn around.

SONG
14

Little stars, that shine so bright,
help to brighten up the night.

Bedtime

Gently lay your sleepy head,
it's time to go to bed.
Daytime light no longer shed,
the stars are out instead.

Twinkle, twinkle, starlight sprinkle,
softly through the air.

Cuddle, cuddle, time to snuggle,
with your teddy bear.

Bedtime stories have been read
and night-nights now are said.
Gently lay your sleepy head
it's time to go to bed.

SONG
15

PART TWO
Music & Lyrics

Barump

♩ = 70

Ba - r - r - r - rump Peem Pom Bom Boom Bom Bay - r - r - r - rump Peem Pom Bom Boom Bom Bay - r - r - r - rump Peem Pom Bom Boom Bom Boom Bom   Bay   Ba - r - r - r

Bay   Oh   Oh   Oh   Oh   Boo - pett - y Poo - py Doo - py   day   Bah - dum Bah - dum Bah - doom Bom Bay   Oh   Oh   Oh   Oh   Boo - pett - y Poo - py doo - py day   Bah

dum Bah - dum Bah - doom Bom Bay - Ba - r - r - r - rump Peem Pom Bom Boom Bom Bay - r - r - r - rump Peem Pom Bom Boom Bom Bay - r - r - rump Peem Pom Bom Boom Bom Boom bom Bay.

Brand New Day

♩ = 67

I   wake up in the morn-ing and I brush my teeth, the front and back top and un - der - neath. I
put   a - way my toys and help to make my bed, then clean my room like my mom - my said. I
pick a pair of pants and then a shirt to match, my fav' - rite socks mom -my needs to patch. I

To Coda

wash my hands and face and eve - y-thing's o - k - get-ting rea-dy for a brand new day.   I   rea-dy for a brand new day.   Cause,
have some toast and jel - ly, then it's time to   play, get - ting
tie   up   both my shoes and then I'm on my way, get - ting

eve - ry - day   is   a   new day.   A fun day   Sky is blue day.   Yes, eve - ry-day's a me and you day,   get - ting

D.S. al Coda   CODA

rea - dy for a brand new day.   I   rea-dy for a brand new day.   get - ting rea-dy for a brand new day!

Family

♩ = 78

Mom - my, Dad - dy, Gram - pa, Gram - my, all a part of fam - i - ly.

Fath - ers, mo - thers, sis - ters, bro - thers, aunts and unc - les, then there's me. A

fam - i - ly gets big - ger, when ba - bies join the world. It's fun to try and fig - ure if it's a boy or girl.

Mom - my, Dad - dy, Gram - pa, Gram - my, all a part of fam - i - ly.

Fath - ers, mo - thers, sis - ters, bro - thers, aunts and unc - les, then there's me!

That's My Doggy

♩ = 139

My dog-gy al-ways pro-tects me, from an-y-one who comes my

go for walks in the af-ter-noon, as soon as I get home from

way. She sits at home with her ball and bone, wait-ing till I'm back to play. That's my

school. She wags her tail as we pick a trail, back for din-ner is the rule.

dog-gy, she's my bud-dy she's my friend. That's my dog-gy, and she'll be here till the end. That's my dog-gy, I'm so

1.
2.

proud to call her mine. That's my dog-gy, so fine! We fine! - That's-my dog-gy, she's my bud-dy she's my friend. That's my

dog-gy, and she'll be here till the end. That's my dog-gy, I'm so proud to call her mine. That's my dog-gy, so fine!

Finger Song

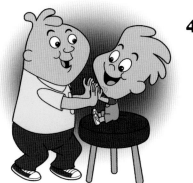

♩ = 86

Fee, fi, fo, fum, Lit - tle, Ring, Mid - dle, Poin - ter, Thumb. - Coun - ting fing - ers one by one, clap your hands and have some fun. - The

Fee, fi, fo, fum, last but not least Mis - ter Thumb. Coun - ting fing - ers one by one, clap your hands and have some fun.

D.S. al Coda

Pink - y is the lit - tle, the Ring is next in line. The long one's in the mid - dle, the Poin - ter then you'll find. clap your hands and have some fun.

rit.

Fee, fi, fo, fum, Lit - tle, Ring, Mid - dle, Poin - ter, Thumb. Coun - ting fing - ers one by one, clap your hands and have some fun!

"Yidel, Deedle, Dydel, Dum."

Daddy's Song

SONG 6

♩ = 80

Lis - ten eve - ry - bo - dy to my Dad - dy's fav' - rite song. Yi - del dee - dle dy - del dum, he sings the whole day long.

Lis - ten eve - ry - bo - dy to my Dad - dy's fav' - rite song. Yi - del dee - dle dy - del dum, it's not so ve - ry long.

Yi - del dee - dle dy - del dum, the words don't mean a thing. Yi - del dee - dle dy - del dum, but hap - pi - ness they bring.

Yi - del dee - dle dy - del dum, will chase a - way the rain. Yi - del dee - dle dy - del dum, on Cher - ry Blos - som Lane.

Yi - del dee - dle dy - del dum, a hap - py mel - o - dy. Yi - del dee - dle dy - del dum, in three part harm - o - ny. Lis - ten eve - ry - bo - dy to my

Dad - dy's fav' - rite song. Yi - del dee - dle dy - del dum, it's fun to sing a - long. Yi - del dee - dle dy - del dum, they're

ma - gic words to say. Yi - del dee - dle dy - del dum, will brigh - ten up your day!

Schooltime

SONG
7

= 124

School Time, School Time. Grab your books and take the bus. School Time, School Time. What a time for all of us.
School Time, School Time. Grab your books and take the bus. School Time, School Time. What a time for all of us.

If you have a thought that's on your mind, put it in a ques-tion then you'll find, raise your hand in class then wait un - til your turn.
If you find your home - work's hard for you, tell ya' what I think you ought to do. See if you can get help from your fam - i - ly.

If you nev - er ask you'll nev - er learn. If you have to do a show and tell, share a stor - y that you know so well. Bring a - long a pic - ture,
You can solve the prob - lem eas- il - y.

or a spe - cial toy. Make it fun for eve - ry girl and boy. School Time, School Time. Grab your books and

take the bus. School Time, School Time. What a time for all of us. What a time for all of us!

Shopping Cart

SONG **8**

♩=71

I like sit-ting in the shop-ping cart, pick-ing food up at the su-per-mart. Mom-my push-es me a-round the store, I find eve-ry-thing we're look-ing for.

First stop's One to get some gum to chew, juice and milk we get on ais-le Two. Fruits and vege-ta-bles on Three and Four. Ais-le Five's be-hind a free-zer door.

Up and down the aisles we go, back and forth and to and fro. Cros-sing off the list we bring, check-ing we don't miss a thing. Next my fav'-rite ais-le num-ber Six,

Up and down the aisles we go, back and forth and to and fro. Cros-sing off the list we bring, check-ing we don't miss a thing.

lots of cook-ies and some pret-zel sticks. Sev-en, Eight, spa-ghet-ti sauce on Nine, down aisle Ten in-to the check-out line. Up and down the aisles we go,

back and forth and to and fro. Cros-sing off the list we bring, check-ing we don't miss a thing. Oh how fun to go shop-ping!

The Playground

SONG
9

= 100

The   play-ground is a place for kids to   run and jump and swing.   The   play-ground is a place for kids to do most an-y-thing. Climb

play-ground is a place for kids to   come and meet new friends.   The   play-ground is a place for kids, the fun just nev-er ends. Swing

1.   2.

way up top the sli-ding pond, then tum-ble to the ground.   If an-y-bod-y wants to know, it's here I can be found. The   why not give a try.-Climb

clear a-cross the Mon-key bars,   a - way up in the sky.   The See-Saw is a game for two, so

way up top   the sli-ding pond, then tum - ble to the ground.   If   an - y - bod - y wants to know, it's here I can be found.   The

play-ground is a place for kids, it's o-pen eve-ry   day.   The play-ground is a place for kids, so come with me and play!

Train Song

♩ = 130

Yee Hee   Hee___   Yee Haw   Ha_____   Yee Hee   Hee___   Ooh___   Ah   Ha_____

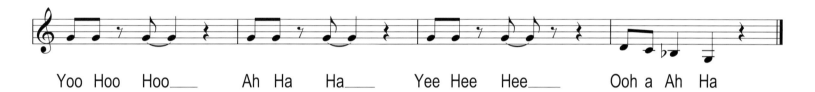

Yoo Hoo   Hoo_____   Ah Ha   Ha_____   Yee Hee   Hee_____   Ooh a   Ah   Ha

My Bicycle

♩ = 128

You may like to   skip - to - my - loo,   or run and jump in   play - school.   But there is one thing   I like to do,

I re - mem - ber   learn - ing to ride,   back when I was   se - ven.   My seat was fat, my   ti - res were wide.

all the live long day through. I   like to ride my   bi - cy - cle.   I   like to ride my bike.

Did I for get to   men - tion?

Bi - cy - cle Rid - er.   I   like to ride my

bi - cy - cle.   I   like to ride my bike.

Owwee

SONG **12**

♩ = 77

Ow - wee Ow - wee oh me - ow - ee, what else can I say?   Ow - wee Ow - wee oh me - ow - ee, make it go a - way. Some

Ow - wee Ow - wee oh me - ow - ee, what else can I say?   Ow - wee Ow - wee oh me - ow - ee, make it go a - way.   So

times you're out - side play - ing,   and   dirt gets in your eye.   A   sting and burn, and then you learn, you

if   you   get   a   boo - boo,   and scrape your hands and knees,   A   sting and burn, and then you learn, be

try   hard   not   to   cry.   Ow - wee   Ow - wee   oh   me - ow - ee,

care - ful   climb - ing   trees.

what else can I   say?   Ow - wee   Ow - wee   oh   me - ow - ee,   make it   go   a - way!

Bubbles

SONG
13

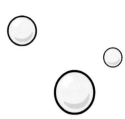

♩ = 67

Bub‑bles, bub‑bles in my tub, they're floa‑ting eve‑ry‑where.   Poke and pop 'em   if you can, be‑fore they dis‑ap‑pear.

Scrub a dub it's fun to wash with   all my friends a‑round.   Here's a small one, there's a tall one.   Shi ‑ ny and so round.

I   like to splish and splash in a bub‑ bly world of snow.   I   like to laugh and play with my duc‑ky and my boat.

I   like   to splish and splash in a bub‑ bly world of snow.   I   like to laugh and play with my duc‑ky and my boat.

What Goes Up

♩ = 65

What goes up, must come down. It's when a smile be-comes a frown. Look at things from up-side down, and they will turn a-round.

My friend Matt had a cat. But then one day she ran a-way. Matt got sad, was fee-ling bad, then his
Cous-in Mike broke his bike. It would-nt ride, and so he cried. Af-ter school, Dad found a tool and
Peg-gy Sue caught the flu, stayed at home and felt a-lone. Her best friend helped her mend and

kit-ty came back to play. What goes up must come down. It's when a smile be-comes a frown.
fixed it's brok en side.
cheered her on the phone.

look at things from up-side down, and they will turn, oh yes they'll turn, and they will turn a-round!

Bedtime

q =58

Gent - ly lay - your - slee - py head - it's time to go to bed. Day - time light no - long - er shed the stars are out in - stead.

Bed - time stor - ies have been read and night - nights now are said. Gent - ly lay your slee - py head it's time to go to bed.

Twin - kle twin - kle star - light sprin - kle soft - ly through the air. Cud - dle cud - dle time to snug - gle with your ted - dy bear.

Twin - kle twin - kle star - light sprin - kle softl - y through the air. Cud - dle cud - dle time to snug - gle with your ted - dy bear.

Bed - time sto - ries heve been read and night - nights have been said. Gent - ly lay - your slee - py head. It's time to go to bed.

Do You Remember?

1. What musical instruments do Leedo and Booey play?
2. Name the family members in the picture frame.
3. What color is Doggy's bow?
4. What is Leedo and Booey's daddy's name?
5. What do the five children play on in the playground?
6. What does Booey like to snuggle with at bedtime?
7. What's the name of Leedo and Booey's choo-choo train?
8. What funny words does daddy sing in his favorite song?
9. Who pushes Leedo and Booey in the shopping cart?
10. Who likes to chase the boys around on the rug?
11. What could you poke and pop while taking a bath?
12. While riding their bicycles, what do the boys have to "KEEP OFF"?
13. What are the names of the fingers in "Fee Fi Fo Fum"?
14. Leedo caught his finger in the _____ .
15. What toys do Leedo and Booey play with in the bath?
16. What color is Leedo and Booey's school bus?
17. Who snores in bed?
18. What is Leedo's favorite ice cream flavor?
19. What do Leedo and Booey put on their toast?
20. What color are the birds in this book?

For the answers, please turn the page.

Answers

1. Flute and trombone
2. Mommy, Daddy, Grampa, Grammy, Leedo and Booey
3. Pink
4. Looey
5. See-saw, monkey bars, sliding pond, swings
6. Teddy Bear
7. Toyville Express
8. Yidel, Deedle, Dydel, Dum.
9. Mommy
10. Doggy
11. Bubbles
12. The grass
13. Little, Ring, Middle, Pointer, Thumb
14. Door
15. Ducky and boat
16. Yellow
17. Leedo
18. Chocolate
19. Jelly
20. Red

Acknowledgments

CD CREDITS:

Music and Lyrics by Dr. Gart
Produced by Dr. Gart

Arrangements by Doug Scott
Engineered by Greg Hainer, Roger Sommers,
John Karr and Doug Scott

Mixed by Noah Snyder
Mastered by Paul du Gre

Vocalists:

Lara Jill Miller	Leedo
Lani Minella	Booey
Dr. Gart	Narrator, Papa Looey, Conductor Bob
DD Howard	Mom

Additional Musicians:

David West	Banjo, Guitar, Bass, and Uke
Glenn Hartman	Accordian
Sheldon Brown	Clarinet
Robby Scharf	Electric Bass
Wally Ingram	Drums and Percussion

BOOK CREDITS:

Sandy Gart	Editor & Creative Director
Layron DeJarnette	Illustrations
PIKE FX	Book Layout & Design
Doug Scott	Music Manuscript

About the Author

Dr. Gart grew up in Merrick, New York and completed his schooling at UCLA Medical Center. His love for music began while learning to play the guitar which still remains his inspiration.

Dr. Gart lives in California with his wife, who he thanks for her love and support.

The fun and music never ends.
Next time 'round you'll meet new friends!